MOTOR RACING
the golden age

MOTOR
the golden

RACING
age

John Tennant

CASSELL
ILLUSTRATED

First published in 2004 by
Cassell Illustrated,
a division of Octopus Publishing Group Limited
2-4 Heron Quays
London E14 4JP

Copyright © John Tennant 2004

Designed by John Tennant and Jack Tennant

The moral right of John Tennant to be
identified as the author of this work has
been asserted in accordance with the
Copyrights, Design and Patents Act of 1988.

Cassell Illustrated acknowledge the
assistance provided by Getty Images

gettyimages

A CIP catalogue record for this book is
available from the British Library.

ISBN 1-84403-203-5

Printed in China.

FOREWORD

'It frequently happens... that the operator himself discovers on examination, perhaps long afterwards, that he had depicted many things he had no notion of at the time'
WILLIAM HENRY FOX TALBOT

'Brakes are no good, they only make you go slower'
TAZIO NUVOLARI

VERY SOON after the automobile was invented at the end of the nineteenth century, it began to attract the attention of photographers, themselves practitioners of a relatively new technology. And when motorists began to claim to be able to drive faster, or more reliably, or over a longer distance, or up a steeper hill, the camera was there to record their endeavours.

This book of motor racing photographs, like my book on football before it, is all about sport and photography – but not about 'sport photography' in its literal sense, and certainly not in its current incarnation of tight long-lens shots with the protagonist filling the frame and the background thrown out of focus. I want to show there is more to photographing sport than 'Chest Breaks Tape', 'Man With Fish' and 'Ball Bursts Net' pictures and that, apart from recording triumph, those photographs often capture little atmosphere and are, ultimately, peripheral, even superficial.

These images represent the golden age of the photography of motor racing; photographs that are about the detail in the seemingly inconsequential, and not fixated on achievement. The current preoccupation with winners suggests that sometimes the best pictures might not be considered for anthologies, although people tend to assume they have been. These photographs are never mere anecdotal illustrations of important events, but images in their own right. And sometimes these images seem to include themselves, as if the collection has a life of its own, insisting on the inclusion of one photograph and denying another.

A considerable number of the images in this book come from a time when clumsy, large-format equipment dictated a more measured approach; a process of composition and consideration, rather than a frenzied, motor-driven response. They reflect a way of looking that seems to have disappeared from the pages of our newspapers and magazines. In the early days of newspaper photography there was no such thing as a specialist sports photographer; they were expected to be able to tackle anything, in the words of the old Daily Express mantra, 'from a sausage to a submarine'. The quality of image produced during this period actually benefits from this wider perspective. Nowadays, press photographers are routinely expected to cover many stories in a day, made possible as the result of all kinds of advances in everyday living, not least in the areas of digital technology and travel. They do not have time to explore all possibilities.

Wherever possible, the photographs are attributed, although most of the old picture agencies operated on the basis that their names, not those of individual photographers, were credited. Consequently, the 'Unknown Photographer' is well represented.

Whilst the book is not bound to a succession of winners it is, most definitely, a slave to research; the hunt for the unusual, unpublished and unknown in archives and libraries. Sometimes this research consisted of sifting through dusty prints or poring over fragile glass negatives, shelved and forgotten for fifty years or more. However grimy this process might be, it remains more fun and potentially more rewarding than the ubiquitous electronic browser. My trawl through the files of the Ludvigsen Library uncovered two wonderful photographs by Rodolfo Mailander; the portrait of Juan Manuel Fangio celebrating victory in the 1950 Monaco Grand Prix (page 258), and Alberto Ascari's beautiful Ferrari 375, casually guarded by an Italian soldier at Monza in 1951 (page 377). Nor would I have discovered the graphic still-life image of a Jaguar C-Type maquette during smoke tunnel testing (pages 42–43), or the group of exhausted competitors napping at Folkestone, after arriving from John O' Groats in the 1937 Monte Carlo Rally, and the jolly alfresco lunch after the 1930 rally (pages 46 and 47).

Before the advent of team racing and works entries, only the wealthy could race motor cars. At Brooklands, the first purpose-built circuit, there was the positive notion that not only were the competitors of a 'certain class', but that spectators should be too. One revealing Brooklands slogan was 'The right crowd and no crowding'. I have tried to capture this cultural and social milieu in the photographs I have selected; likewise, the spirit and sense of fun of the colourful personalities who graced the sport before it became the high-speed procession of advertising hoardings we see today.

Motor Racing The Golden Age is neither narrative nor comprehensive history; it is an Aladdin's cave. I have not worked from a list of celebrated drivers, cars or races: instead I have surrendered to the power of each image to claim its place. So there are no chequered flags to be found here (and only a solitary example of post-race champagne-swigging). But there is lots of accidental and unintentional beauty, maybe a tiny detail, on the periphery of whatever was intended to be the focus of attention, sufficient to mark out a picture and transform the potentially mundane into something extraordinary and memorable. JOHN TENNANT

INTRODUCTION
by Sir Jackie Stewart OBE

OTORSPORT IS THE SHARP END of the technology of the motor industry, the world's third largest manufacturing industry. The motor vehicle is here to stay, as there is no viable alternative in the foreseeable future for the transportation of people or goods. Whatever we do on water, in the air or on railways, the motor vehicle will be with us for a very long time to come. Men and women will therefore continue to be magnetically compelled to take the motor vehicle to the absolute limits of its ability.

Motor racing seems to have been something of a magnet for photographers as well. The challenge – particularly in the early days of photography – to capture the images of speed with clarity created a band of enthusiasts who followed the motorsporting calendar around the world. The drama and the danger of motorsport was often graphically reproduced around the world by the motorsporting photographic corps. This book pays tribute as much to the skills of those photographers as it does to the sport. The great and the good are highlighted, their achievements and their innovations preserved for future generations. Sometimes the bizarre also features, such as the photograph of the 500cc Cooper perched on the roof of what is almost certainly a disused army building at Blandford in Dorset, where ironically my racing driver brother Jimmy Stewart served part of his Army National Service duties.

I don't know whether it is part of the process of growing older, but when I look at these photographs of motorsport, which spread over a great number of years, I don't look at what most people see as the feature or the centre of the photographer's attention, but I look in the background to see if I can recognise any of the folks who were part and parcel of the world of motorsport over the years. Many of them might have been journalists or photographers themselves, mechanics, engineers, wives or girlfriends of drivers, or part of the technology teams of the many companies whose products were developed and demonstrated in motorsport.

Motorsport has developed into an extremely successful cottage industry for the United Kingdom. Many nations have enjoyed windows of great influence and success over the years – France, Germany, Italy and, significantly in more modern times, Great Britain. Britain did have success in the nineteen-twenties, thirties and fifties in land speed record attempts with men such as Seagrave, Campbell and Cobb, and the Bentley Boys waved the Union Flag with great pride at their many successes at Le Mans. But it wasn't until the late fifties and early sixties that the sport's busiest development activities moved from their traditional home of Italy to Britain.

The rear-engined car was re-introduced to motorsport by John Cooper and Colin Chapman. Their little single-seater mid-engined racing cars, with the driver positioned ahead of the engine, created a dominance that brought enormous prestige to British racing. These two men are largely responsible for the creation of the British motorsports industry developing into one of the most significantly successful clusters that the world has known. Motorsport has been probably the only manufacturing industry in Britain that has steadily

progressed and grown on an annual basis since the end of World War II. BRM and Vanwall, Jaguar and Aston Martin, Riley and MG, Fraser Nash and many others all played a part in planting the seeds that were to produce the machinery and the people who are featured in the upcoming pages.

Motor racing is colourful, it is glamorous and it is exciting. This book elegantly and definitively illustrates the many facets of what is now a global sport that is more popular today than ever before. It has captured the imagination and the passion of men and women in almost every corner of the world. The carmakers, the tyre makers, the fuel and oil producers and the many other component areas that make up the racing car and what goes with it, have been intoxicated and driven to be part of this wonderful kaleidoscope of life that motorsport is - and this book has been created to celebrate it.

SIR JACKIE STEWART OBE

Jackie Stewart (Matra MS 10 Ford) during the 1968 German Grand Prix at the Nurburgring. Rain and fog had produced near-zero visibility on a deadly track. But Stewart led by eight seconds after the first lap and by over four minutes at the end

George Abecassis (ERA) during the
Swedish Winter Grand Prix, which was
run on the frozen Lake Vallentuna.
February 1947. Photographer not known

Alberto Ascari (Lancia D24) is carried through the crowd after winning the Mille Miglia. He is led by Lancia team manager Attilo Pasquarelli, who carries Ascari's precious blue crash helmet. **May 1954.** Photograph by Rodolfo Mailander

Temporary chicanes during the
JCC International Trophy Race at Brooklands.
1936. Photographer not known

Giuseppe 'Nino' Farina demonstrates a rain-deflecting visor. 1951.
Photograph by Rodolfo Mailander

Opposite: Jim Clark watches the qualifying rounds for the British Grand Prix at Brands Hatch. July 1966. Photograph by Victor Blackman

The start of the Vanderbilt Cup Motor Race. Santa Monica, California. March 1914. Photographer not known

The start of the 100 Miles Race. Indianapolis, Indiana. Circa 1910. Photograph by Paul Thompson

Mannin Beg competitors pass through Douglas, Isle of Man. May 1934. Photographer not known

Salvador Fabregas (Mercedes 300SL) in the Monte Carlo Rally. 1956. Photographer not known

Timekeeper at Bramshott Motor Trials, Hampshire. September 1919. Photograph by Roper

Timekeepers on Magilligan Strand, Irish Automobile Club Reliability Trials. November 1907. Photographer not known

Clerk of the course Charles Faroux addresses
competitors before the Monaco Grand Prix.
Foreground left to right: Philippe Etancelin, Antonio
Brivio, Tazio Nuvolari, Rene Dreyfus, Giuseppe
Farina, Rudolf Caracciola, Earl Howe, Luigi Fagioli,
Raymond Sommer, Charles Faroux and Goffredo
Zehender. April 1935. Photographer not known

Stirling Moss wins the United States Grand Prix. Riverside, California.
November 1960. Photographer not known

Opposite: Bruce Maclaren wins the United States Grand Prix. Sebring, Florida.
December 1959. Photographer not known

Hugh Hunter in his Frazer Nash–BMW during the MCC Edinburgh Time Trial. 1938. Photographer not known

W. A. Carr drives down Blackwell Hill, Derbyshire, during the ACC Six Day Reliability Trials. August 1926. Photograph by H. F. Davis

Kaye Don takes a trial run in the
ice-cooled 'Silver Bullet' before
his land speed record attempt at
Daytona Beach, Florida. March 1930.

Mille Miglia.
1952. Photograph by Rodolfo Mailander

Opposite: Supercharged 1.5 litre NSU team after taking 1st, 2nd, 3rd and 4th position in their class in the German Grand Prix. Avus. 1926. Photographer not known

Fangio leads Moss (both Mercedes W196) through the high-speed banked curves at Monza in the Italian Grand Prix. September 1955. Photographer not known

Opposite: Moss (Vanwall VW5) is congratulated by Fangio after winning the Italian Grand Prix at Monza. September 1957. Photographer not known

Irish Automobile Club Reliability Trials.
May 1908. Photographer not known

Joan Richmond and Kay Petre overhaul their Riley. October 1933. Photographer not known

Opposite: Mrs E. Gordon-Simpson and Joan Richmond compose themselves before a race. July 1934. Photographer not known

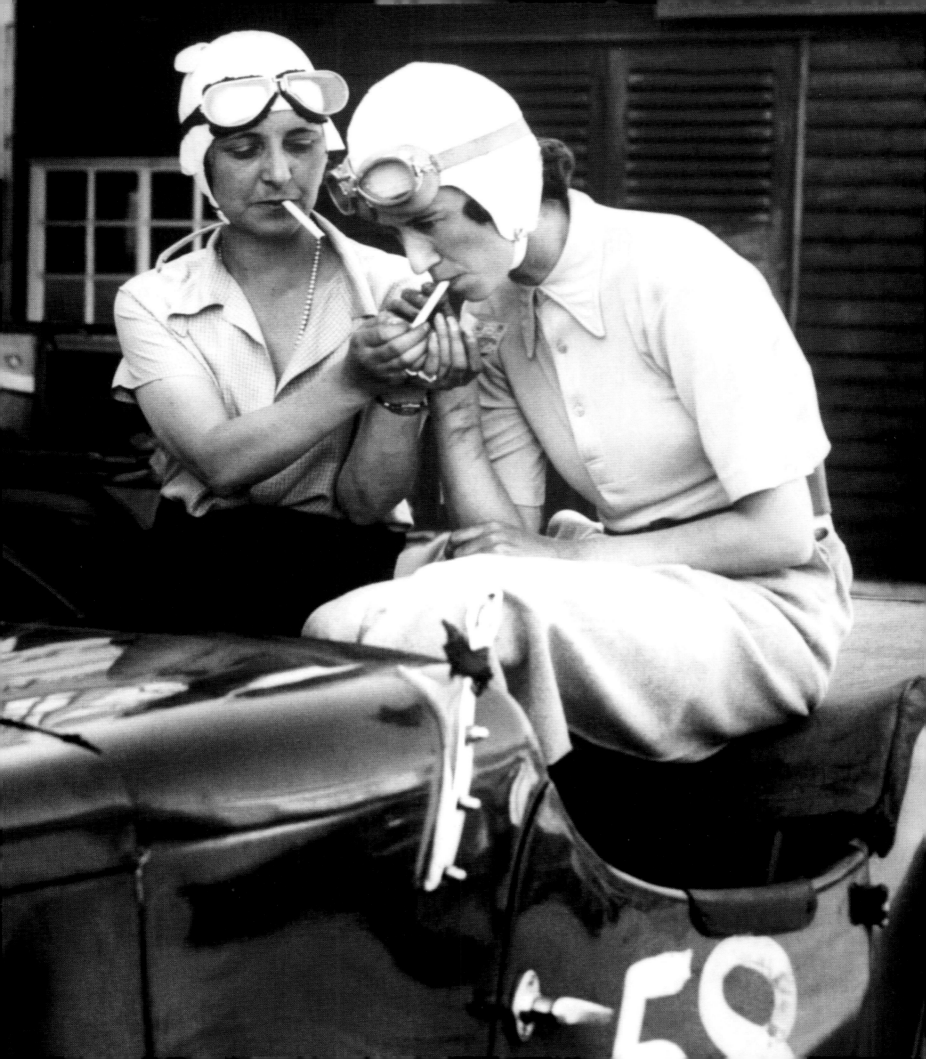

The Jaguar C-Type prototype model undergoes smoke tunnel testing. 1952. Photographer not known

Scottish Trials. June 1906.
Photographer not known

Monte Carlo Rally competitors recuperate after arriving at Folkestone from John O'Groats. January 1937. Photographer not known

Contestants recuperate after completing the Monte Carlo Rally. 1930. Photographer not known

Peter Whitehead (Jaguar D-Type) celebrates victory in the Reims
12 Hour Race. July 1954. Photograph by Vachon

Opposite: Jo Siffert invents champagne spraying as
celebration after Dan Gurney and A. J. Foyt's victory in the
Le Mans 24 Hour Race. June 1967. Photographer not known

MCC Land's End Trial.
1934.
Photographer not known

Alan Whicker and Helen Stewart as she times her husband during practice. September 1972. Photographer not known

Opposite: Jackie Stewart at Brands Hatch for the qualifying of the British Grand Prix. July 1972. Photographer not known

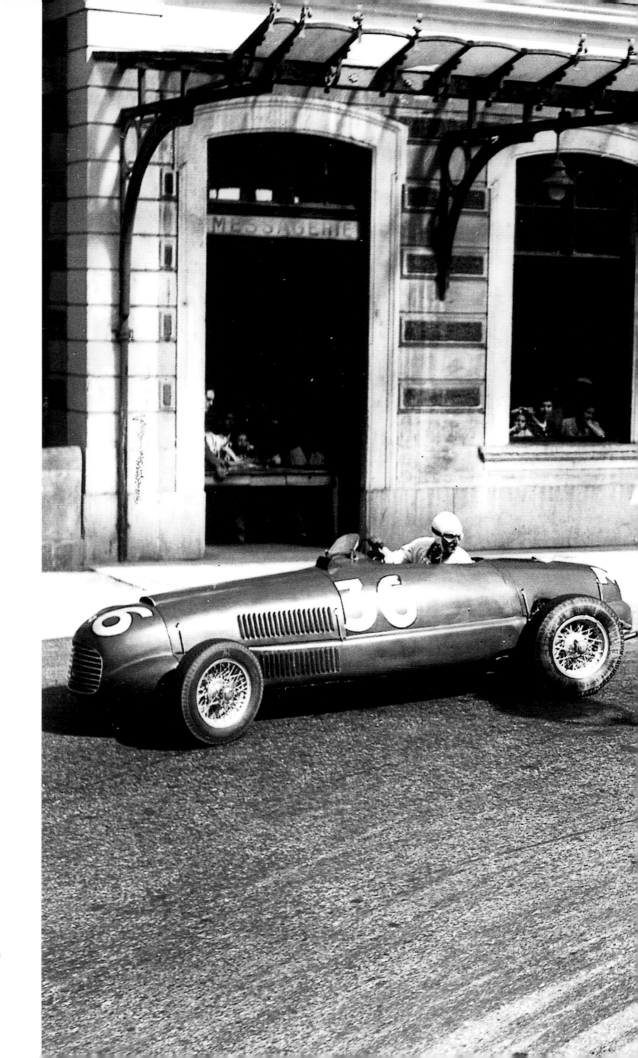

Yves Giraud-Cabantous (Lago Talbot 150C) prepares to pass Count Igor Troubetskoy (Ferrari 166SC) in the Monaco Grand Prix. May 1948. Photographer not known

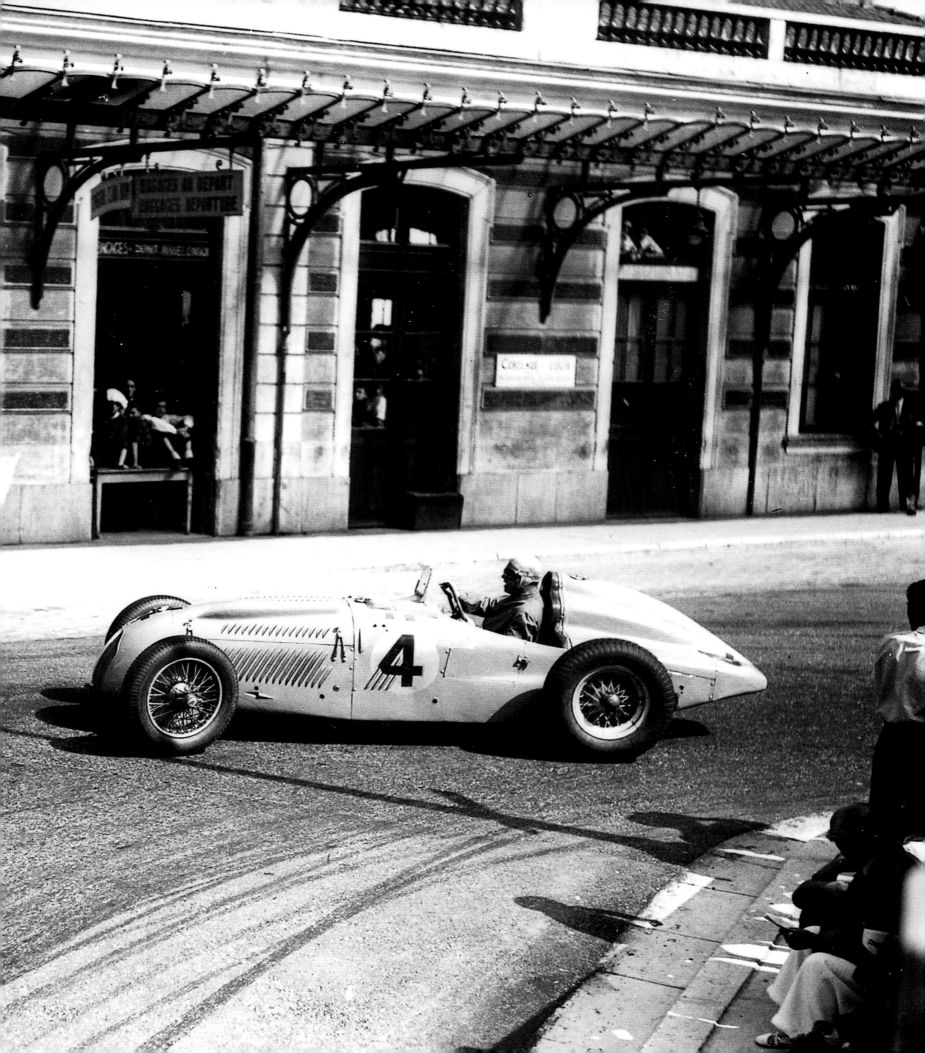

John Cobb with his new Napier Railton at Brooklands. March 1934. Photographer not known

Opposite: John Cobb. 1934. Photographer not known

Starting grid at the Leighton Buzzard Derby Day races. July 1952. Photograph by Ronald Startup

Opposite: Preparing for a 'soap-box' race. Leighton Buzzard. July 1952. Photograph by Ronald Startup

Preceding page: Troy Rottman (right) surprises Andy Linden (left) in the Indianapolis 500. 1954. Photograph by O'Dell & Shields Studios

**Malcolm Campbell in his 350 hp
Sunbeam at Pendine Sands,
Carmarthen, Wales, before
reaching 146.16 mph to break the
land speed record. September 1924.**
Photographer not known

G. Ansell (ERA) at Silverstone, Northamptonshire. October 1948. Photograph by Denis Oulds

A. Owen (Cooper) at Oulton Park, Cheshire. September 1959. Photographer not known

Mike Hawthorn at Aintree for the British Grand Prix. July 1955. Photographer not known

Opposite: Mike Hawthorn (Lancia Ferrari 801) during the Monaco Grand Prix. May 1957. Photographer not known

Carroll Shelby (Aston Martin
DBR1/30) during the Le Mans
24 Hour Race. June 1959.
Photograph by Edward Eves

The Great West Motor Club Haward Tanker Trial at Camberly Heath. January 1936. Photograph by E. Dean

Hill climb at Freak Hill near Bradford. May 1927. Photographer not known

Jack Brabham watches the Dutch Grand Prix. July 1965.
Photograph by Victor Blackman

Opposite: Jack Brabham and Charles Cooper with Jayne Mansfield.
Riverside, California. November 1960. Photographer not known

Manfred Von Brauchitsch (Mercedes W125) at Donington Park. October 1937. Photographer not known

Alfa Romeo designer Gioacchino Colombo and driver Emmanuel 'Toulo' de Graffenried display a team poster anticipating victory in the Spanish Grand Prix. Fangio (Alfa 159) won the race. October 1951. Photographer not known

Opposite: Luigi Bertett, President of the Automobile Club in Milan and Enzo Ferrari at Monza. September 1953. Photograph by Rodolfo Mailander

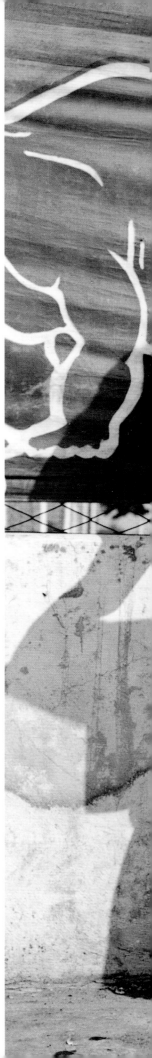

Jean Reville's racing car, 'The Gnat', is claimed to be the smallest in the world. April 1935. Photograph by R. Wesley

Opposite: Sig Haugdahl breaks the standing mile record in 22.6 seconds at Pablo Beach, Florida. His car, which is 20 inches at its widest point, has an engine, originally intended for a hydroplane, that weighs only 600 lb. March 1922. Photographer not known

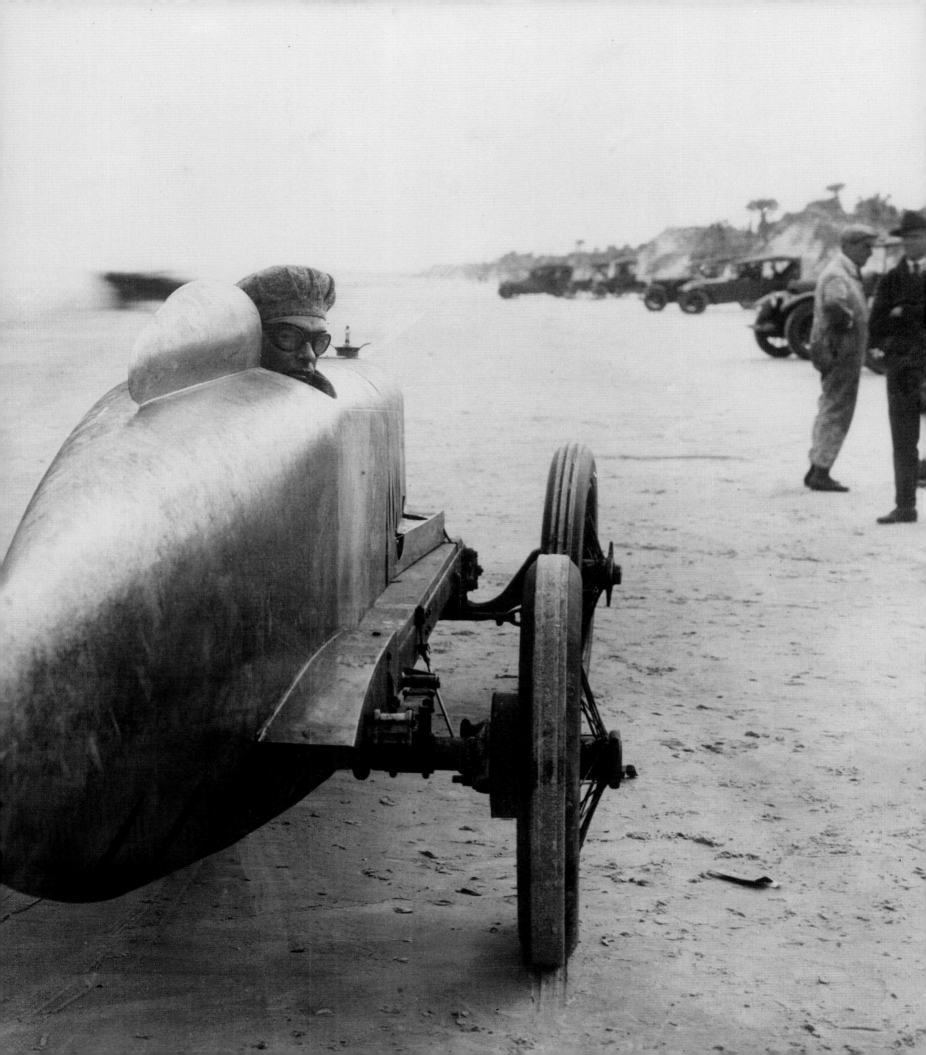

Maurice Trintignant's Bugatti 251 with its 'straight 8' engine. Forced to retire from the French Grand Prix with a broken accelerator after 18 laps, this was the last time Bugatti took part in Formula 1. June 1956.

Byfleet Bridge at Brooklands during the JCC Double Twelve Hour Race. May 1931. Photographer not known

Peter Collins. Monaco Grand Prix. May 1956. Photographer not known

Opposite: Alfonso de Portago in his Lancia-Ferrari D50. French Grand Prix. June 1956. Photographer not known

Marcel Lehoux (Bugatti T54) retires with transmission failure from the French Grand Prix at Reims. July 1932.
Photographer not known

Six Day Trial. Location not known. Circa 1900s. Photographer not known

Opposite: Isle of Man Tourist Trophy. 1914. Photographer not known

British Grand Prix at Silverstone.
July 1956. Photograph by Bert Hardy

John Parry Thomas in
'Babs' and Miss Anne Duke
Williams in her vehicle.
April 1925. Photographer
not known

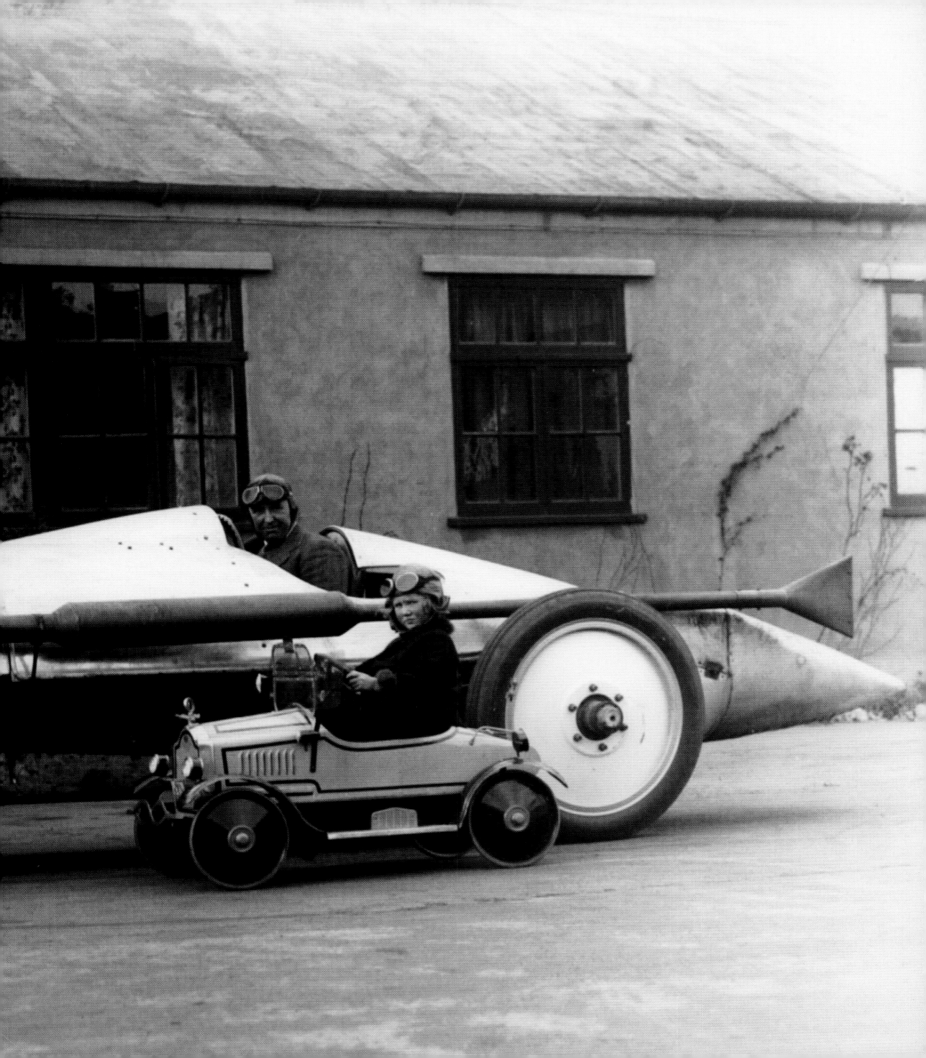

Jacky Ickx waits while mechanics work on his car. Brands Hatch. July 1970.
Photographer not known

Opposite: Stirling Moss has the sole of his shoe cleaned. Location not known. 1953.
Photograph by Ronald Startup

Arthur Waite and the Earl of March receive pit
instructions during the British Double Twelve Hour Race
at Brooklands. May 1930. Photographer not known

Goldie Gardner (Aston Martin Ulster) at the Le Mans 24 Hour Race. June 1935. Photographer not known

S. C. H. Davies' car in the Easter Meeting at Brooklands. April 1931. Photograph by Douglas Miller

Fangio is congratulated by his partner, Andreina 'Beba' Espinosa, after winning the German Grand Prix. August 1956. Photographer not known

Opposite: Fangio and Beba in the Mercedes presented to him by the company on his retirement from racing. August 1958. Photographer not known

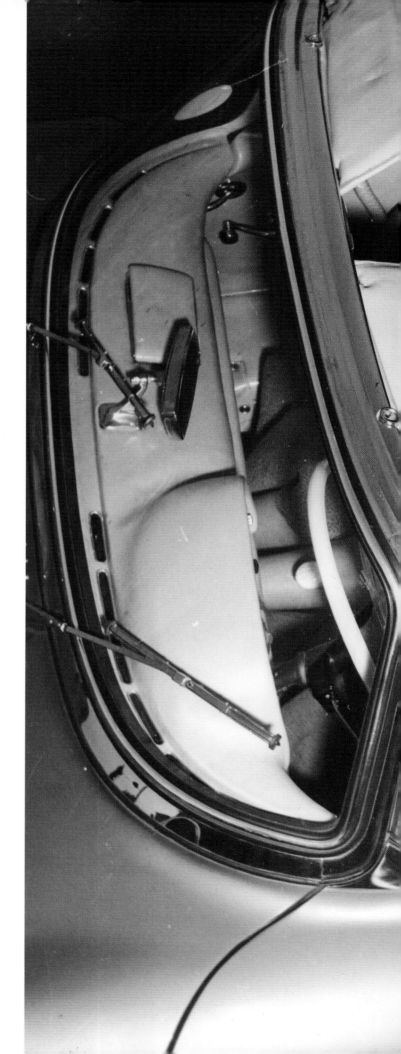

P. C. Wheeler's Alfa Romeo is helped to the top of Crowell Hill in Oxfordshire during the Inter-Varsity Trials. Circa 1925. Photograph by W. J. Brunell

Captain George Eyston's 73-litre twin Rolls-Royce-engined 'Thunderbolt'
before setting a land speed record of 357.5 mph on Bonneville Salt Flats, Utah.
July 1938. Photographer not known

An unknown reserve driver at the Ards circuit for the Ulster Tourist Trophy.
September 1936. Photograph by J. Smith

Opposite: Willy Mairesse watches the Nurburgring 1000 Km from the pits.
1962. Photographer not known

The Gambetta Bend on the
seafront circuit at Nice. 1947.
Photographer not known

Bank Holiday meeting at Brooklands. August 1928. Photographer not known

Spectators on the River Wey watch the racing at Brooklands. August 1938. Photographer not known

Jackie Stewart promotes Hallmark Tapes in Woolworths.
November 1973. Photographer not known

Opposite: Jackie Stewart promotes Dunlop tyres.
July 1969. Photographer not known

Freddie Dixon (Riley) at the Ulster Tourist Trophy.
September 1932. Photographer not known

Opposite: Culver City Speedway, Los Angeles.
November 1924. Photographer not known

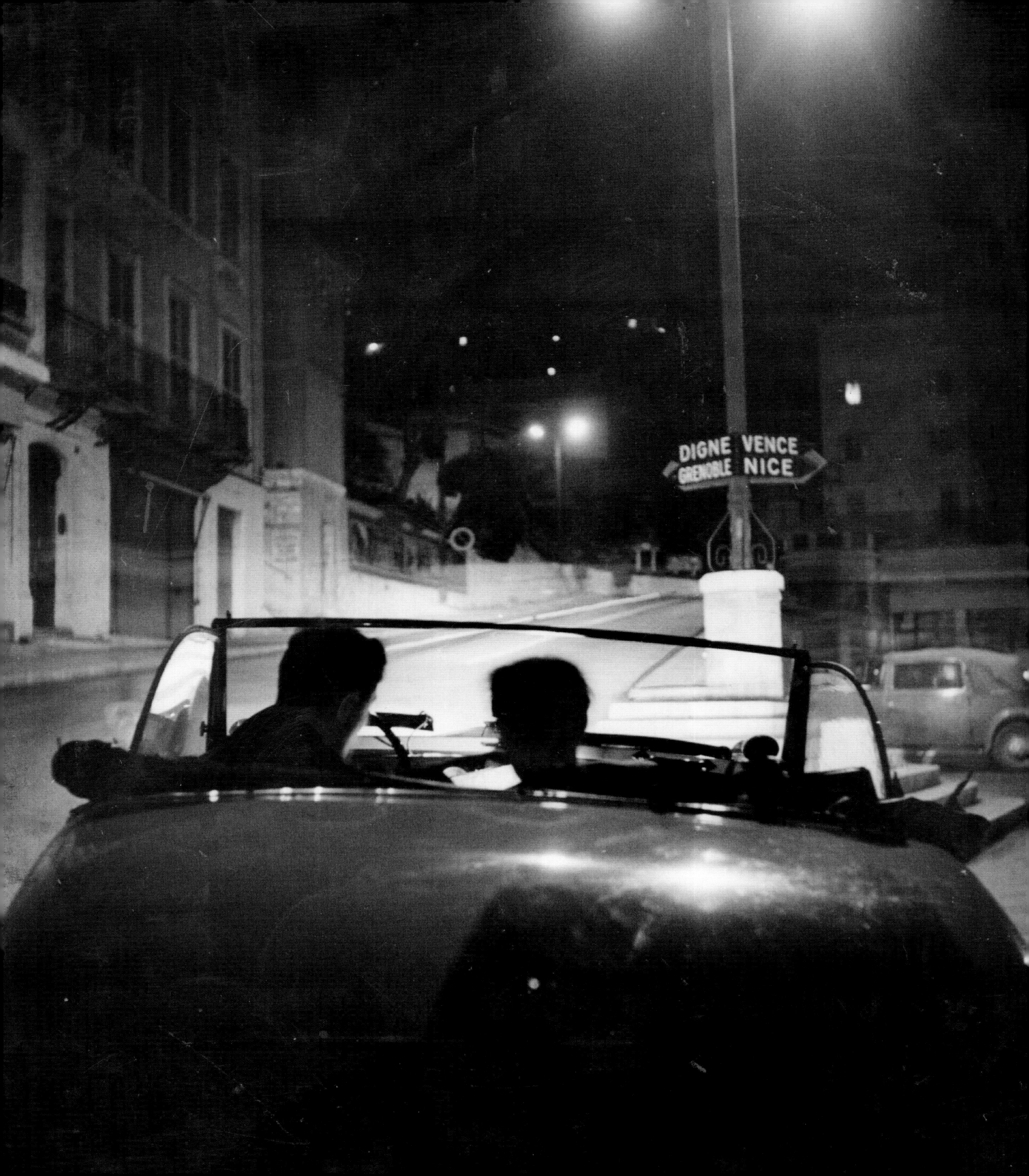
DIGNE VENCE
GRENOBLE NICE

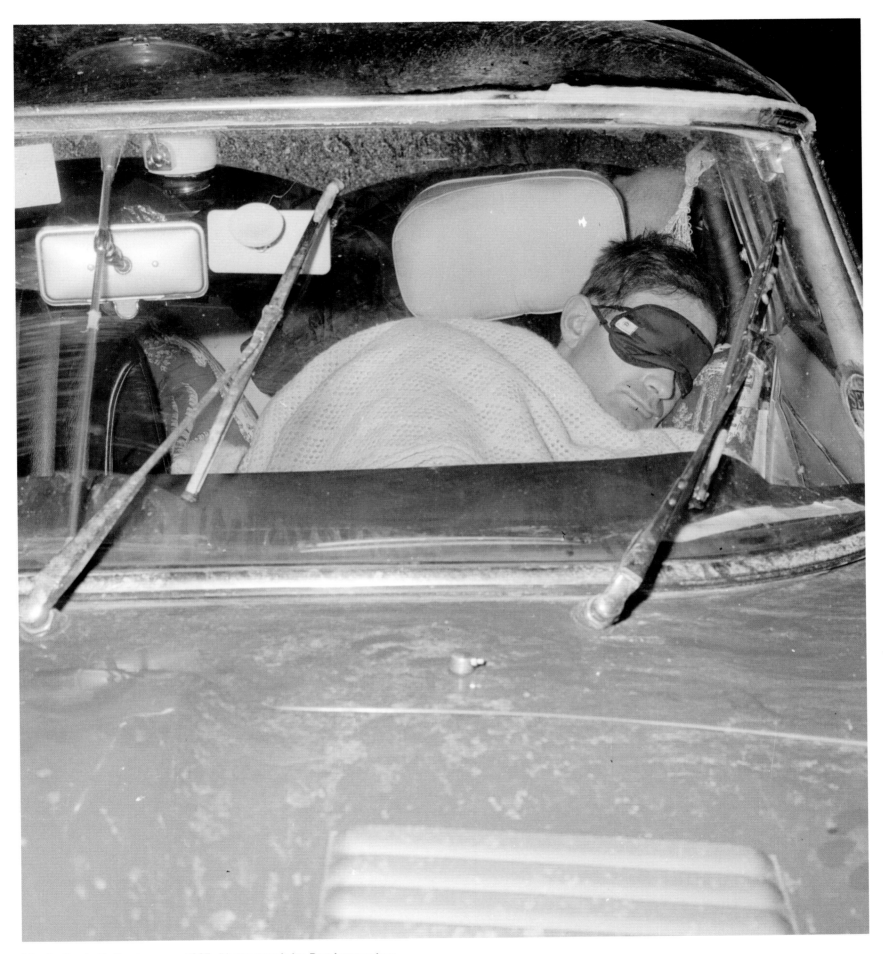

Monte Carlo Rally. January 1963. Photograph by Reg Lancaster

Opposite: Monte Carlo Rally. January 1949. Photographer not known

Jack Dunfee (Bentley)
during the 500 Miles Race
at Brooklands.
October 1931. Photograph
by Francis M. R. Hudson

Tazio Nuvolari wins the RAC Tourist Trophy at Ards. August 1930. Photographer not known

Opposite: Tazio Nuvolari. Circa 1930. Photograph by Max Schirmer

Reg Parnell's Connaught at Crystal
Palace. 1956. Photographer not known

The 28.3–litre Fiat S76 that attained 180 mph at Long Island, USA. 1912. Photographer not known

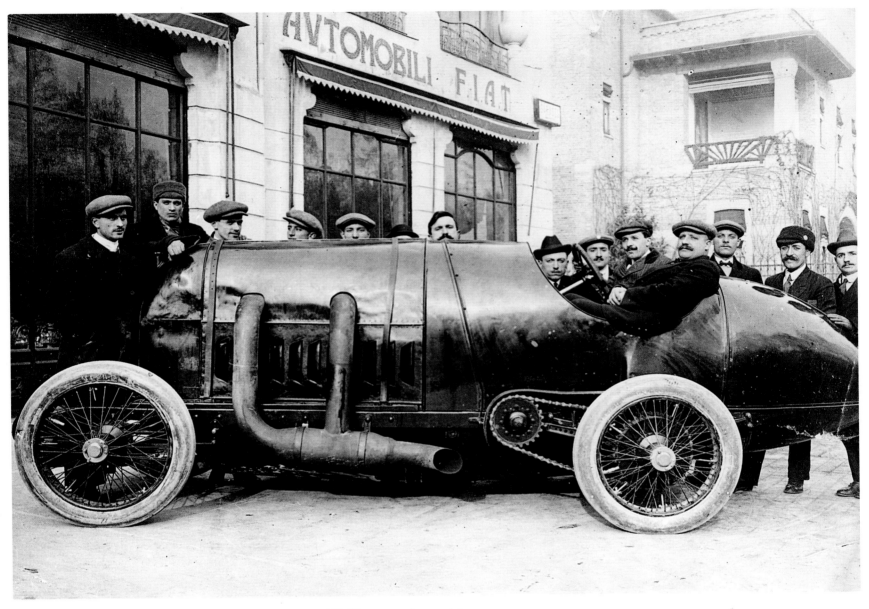

300 hp Fiat racing car fitted with 'street mufflers'. 1911. Photographer not known

Maria Teresa de Filippis (Maserati 250F), non-qualifier for the Monaco Grand Prix. May 1958. Photographer not known
Opposite: 'Racing motorist' the Honourable Mrs Victor Bruce. February 1930. Photographer not known

Sir Henry Birkin (Alfa Romeo 8C)
emerges from Dundonald Bridge during
the RAC Tourist Trophy at Ards.
August 1932. Photographer not known

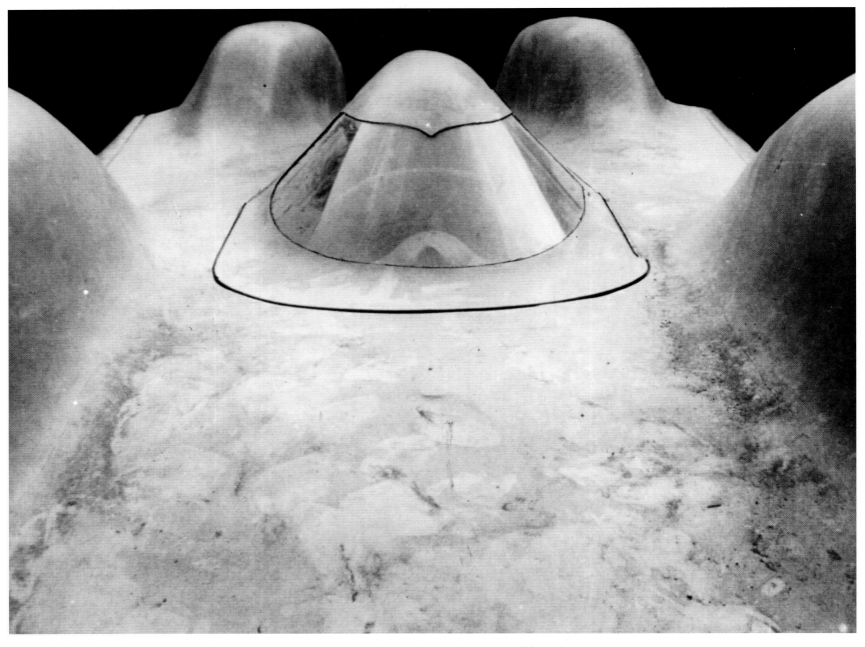

Cockpit of the 3000 hp Mercedes Benz, developed to attempt the land speed record, with an anticipated speed of up to 450 mph. November 1945. Photographer not known

Opposite: Bernd Rosemeyer, driving an Auto Union C-Type, sets a new flying mile record of 252.46 mph on an autobahn near Frankfurt. October 1937. Photographer not known

Ascari (Ferrari 125)
at Valentino Park, Turin.
April 1950. Photograph by
Rodolfo Mailander

The 'Virage des Sept Chemins' hairpin in the French Grand Prix at Lyons. August 1924. Photographer not known

Opposite: Felix Nazzano (2 litre supercharged Fiat) and his mechanic after winning the
French Grand Prix at Strasbourg. Maintaining an average speed of 78.9 mph over the 500 miles of the race,
he finished 57 minutes ahead of the next car. September 1922. Photographer not known

Fiat's Lingotto factory in Turin has
a rooftop racetrack. December 1929.
Photographer not known

The first BRM is unveiled at Folkingham, Lincolnshire.
May 1950. Photograph by Haywood Magee

Opposite: Mechanics make final adjustments to the first BRM.
May 1950. Photograph by Haywood Magee

Willy Mairesse (Ferrari Dino 246) in the Italian Grand Prix at Monza.
September 1960. Photographer not known

Opposite: The North Curve at the Avus circuit during the German Grand Prix.
August 1959. Photographer not known

Prince Scipone Borghese, Luigi Barzini and mechanic Ettore Guizzardi beside the open-top Itala that won the 9936-mile Peking to Paris race. It took two months to complete the course. China. **June 1907.** Photographer not known

Mr J. L. M. Meikle with his self-built jet-propelled racing car. Bangor, Wales. January 1957. Photograph by McMillan

Opposite: Rocket-propelled car. Circa 1930. Photographer not known

Jim Clark and Lotus team manager Colin Chapman at Brands Hatch.
July 1964. Photographer not known

Opposite: Jim Clark and Colin Chapman inspect a Ferrari Dino 156 at the
Nurburgring. August 1962. Photographer not known

Froilan Gonzales (Ferrari) is
signalled to take it easy by Fangio,
who is spectating trackside.
Pescara. August 1951.
Photographer not known

Following page: Headlight trails
in the Monte Carlo Rally. 1966.
Photographer not known

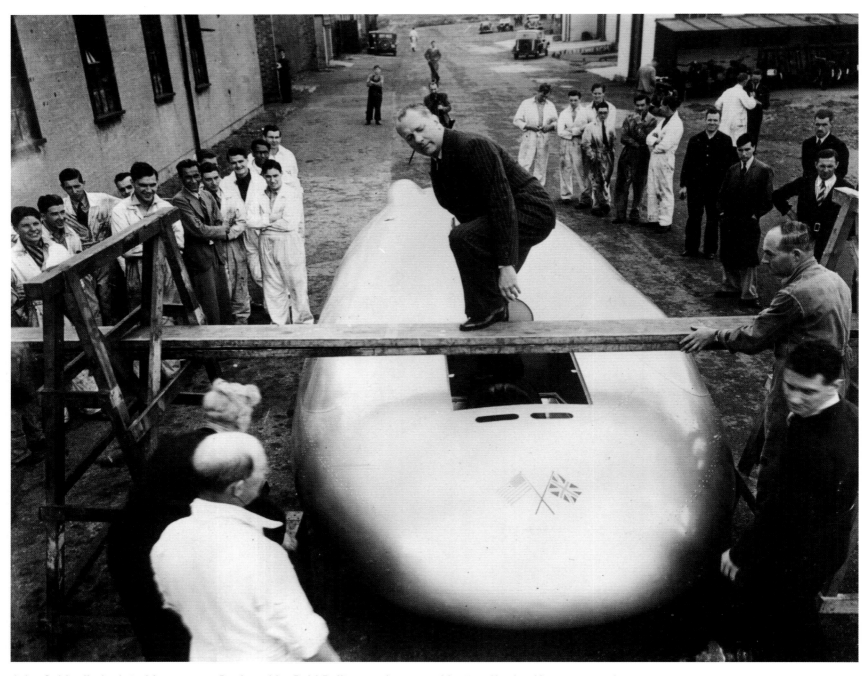

John Cobb climbs into his new car. Designed by Reid Railton and powered by two Napier Lion aero engines, it produces 2500 hp. July 1938. Photograph by David Savill

John Cobb at the wheel of his Railton Mobil Special, shortly before setting a new land speed record of 394.2 mph at Bonneville. August 1947. Photograph by J. A. Hampton

Indianapolis 500. May 1964. Photograph by Jack Wingert

Farina leads Ascari (both Ferrari 500), Fangio and Marimon (both Maserati A6GCM) in the Italian Grand Prix at Monza. September 1953. Photographer not known

Opposite: Fangio followed by Farina and Marimon in the Italian Grand Prix at Monza. September 1953. Photographer not known

Speed record meeting on
Saltburn Sands, Yorkshire. June
1922. Photographer not known

Giuseppe 'Nino' Farina after winning the British Grand Prix at Silverstone.
May 1950. Photograph by Denis Oulds

Opposite: Farina at the Nurburgring. July 1951. Photograph by Rodolfo Mailander

Gill Scott in her Leyland-Thomas at
Brooklands for the Surbiton Motor Club races.
July 1927. Photographer not known

Freddie Dixon has the steering adjusted on his car before the 500 Miles Race
at Brooklands. September 1936. Photograph by William Vanderson

Opposite: A student examines a Porsche 550 Spyder at the annual race-driving school
at Campione, Switzerland. April 1955. Photograph by Rodolfo Mailander

Team manager Alfred Neubauer celebrates with Stirling Moss and his father, after Moss signs to race for Mercedes. January 1955.
Photograph by Bert Hardy

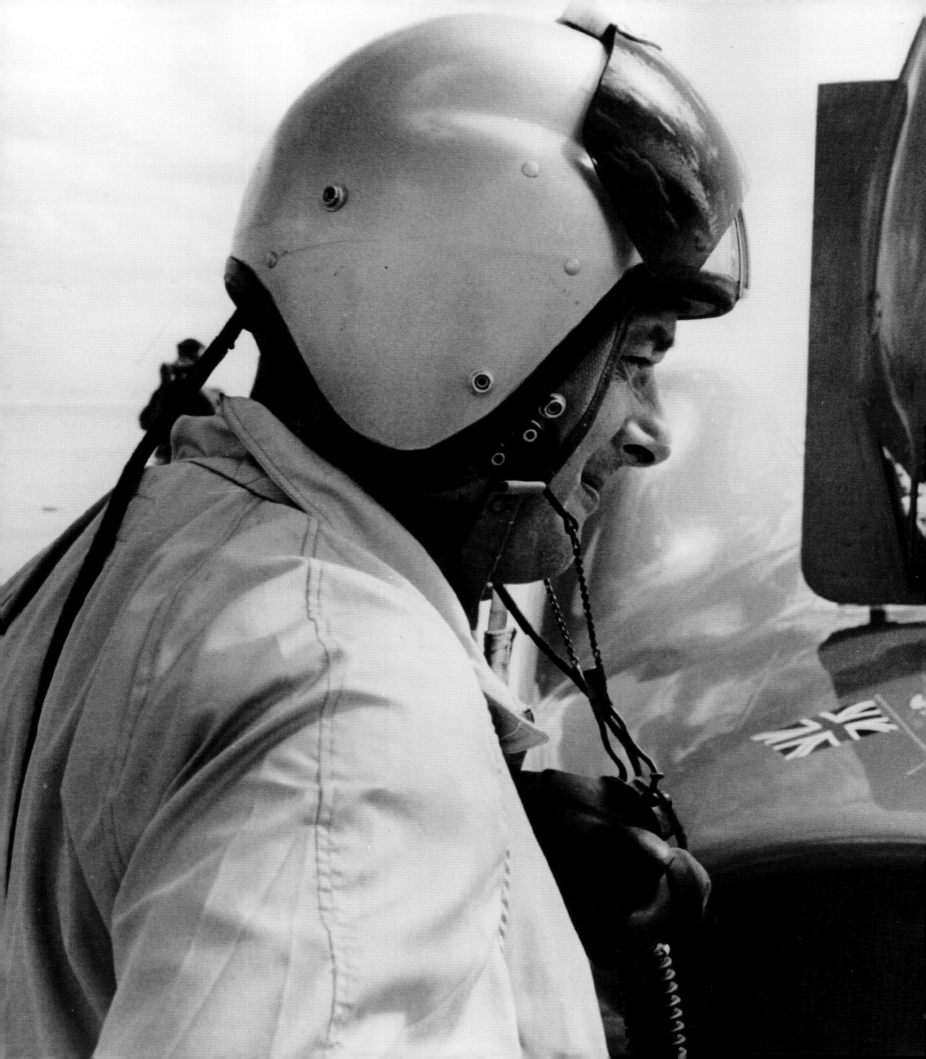

Donald Campbell's 'Bluebird' at Goodwood before leaving for a land speed record attempt at Bonneville, Utah. July 1960. Photograph by Harry Todd

Opposite: Donald Campbell at Lake Eyre, Australia, before setting a new land speed record of 403.1 mph. July 1964. Photographer not known

Pedal car Grand Prix at Crystal Palace. June 1967. Photographer not known

Hill climb at Shelsley Walsh, Worcestershire. 1947. Photographer not known
Opposite: Surbiton Club hill climb. 1924. Photographer not known

Spectators spill on to the track at the Argentinian Grand Prix. February 1950.
Photographer not known

Lincoln Beachey's aeroplane races Barney Oldfield's car in Los Angeles. February 1914. Photographer not known

Juan Manuel Fangio (Alfa Romeo 158) during the Monaco Grand Prix. May 1950. Photographer not known

Opposite: Rudolf Caracciola (Mercedes SSK) during the Monaco Grand Prix. April 1929. Photographer not known

Richie Ginther discusses the new Honda V12 RA273 with his mechanics at the Italian Grand Prix at Monza. September 1966. Photograph by Maxwell Boyd

Opposite: Honda mechanics make final adjustments to the V12 before the Italian Grand Prix at Monza. September 1966. Photograph by Reg Lancaster

Le Mans 24 Hour Race. June 1930.
Photographer not known

Jim Clark judges the Miss England beauty contest.
April 1966. Photograph by Clive Limpkin

Opposite: Graham Hill is 'Miss Earth'.
November 1966. Photograph by Victor Blackman

Adolf Hitler sends a wreath for Dick Seaman, who was killed driving in heavy rain at the Belgian Grand Prix. London. June 1939. Photograph by A. J. O'Brien

Opposite: Dick Seaman (Mercedes) on the podium after winning the German Grand Prix at the Nurburgring. July 1938. Photograph by George Monkhouse

Before the start of the Indianapolis 500. 1912. Photographer not known

Pierre Levegh (Mercedes 300 SLR) at Le Mans immediately before his fatal crash. June 1955. Photograph by Bert Hardy

Opposite: The aftermath of Levegh's accident at Le Mans. 83 people were killed and 75 injured. June 1955. Photographer not known

George Eyston's MG makes
a speed record attempt
at Brooklands. March 1931.
Photographer not known

Kitty Brunell prepares her Talbot 14/45 for the Monte Carlo Rally. October 1929. Photographer not known

Kitty Brunell tunes her engine. June 1932. Photographer not known

Ferrari fans during the Italian Grand Prix at Monza.
September 1953. Photograph by Ronald Startup

Opposite: Jim Clark followed by Jackie Stewart,
Graham Hill and Dan Gurney drift through the Parabolica
in the Italian Grand Prix at Monza. September 1965.
Photographer not known

Earl Howe during the Double Twelve Hour Race at Brooklands. May 1929.
Photographer not known

198

Fangio (Alfa Romeo 159) during the Swiss Grand Prix at Bremgarten. May 1951. Photographer not known

Opposite: Fangio (Maserati 250F) during the German Grand Prix at the Nurburgring. August 1957. Photographer not known

Raymond Mays' first car. Circa 1908. Photographer not known

Raymond Mays in his Bugatti at Porthcawl Sands. Circa 1923. Photographer not known

C. H. Wood climbs the Col du Galibier in his Aston Martin. August 1933. Photographer not known

The inaugural meeting at Brooklands. July 1907. Photographer not known

Opposite: Malcolm Campbell supervises construction of the 'road circuit' at Brooklands.
March 1937. Photograph by Fred Morley

Graham Hill wins the
United States Grand Prix at
Watkins Glen. October 1965.
Photograph by Stanley Rosenthall

Boy Scouts on scoreboard duty at Brooklands. August 1922. Photographer not known

French Grand Prix at Lyons. July 1914. Photographer not known

Juan Manuel Fangio pays his respects at the grave of Alberto Ascari. Killed during a trial run at Monza, Ascari is buried in the family tomb, beside his racing driver father Antonio, in Milan. June 1955. Photographer not known

Opposite: Stirling Moss and Fangio at Pierre Levegh's funeral in Paris, after the Le Mans tragedy. June 1955. Photographer not known

Ferrari workshop in Maranello, Italy. September 1950. Photograph by Rodolfo Mailander

Opposite: Jaguar's experimental department at work on a prototype D-Type. 1954. Photographer not known

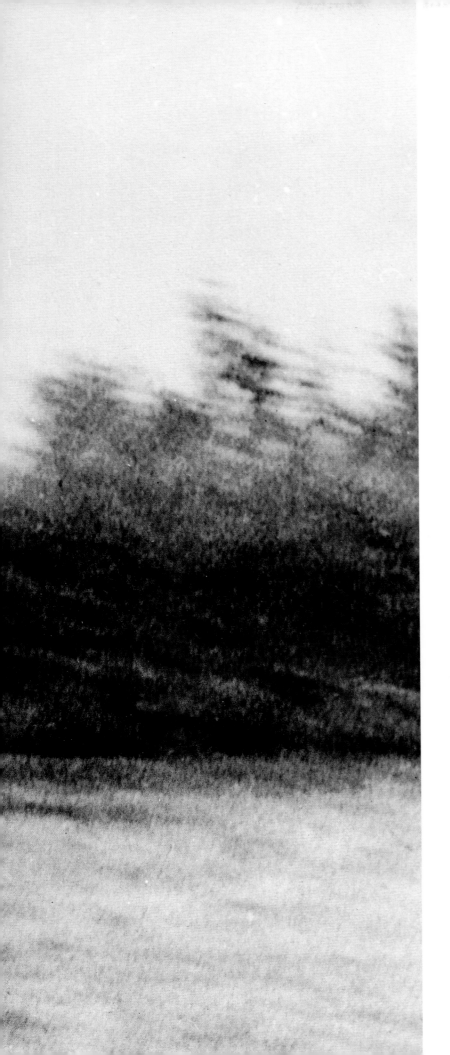

Above and opposite: Paul Pietsch (Alfa Romeo 159) loses control on the North Curve at the Nurburgring during the German Grand Prix. His car spins, then leaps into the air, before crashing down into the road below. He is unhurt and attempts to explain what happened to the Alfa mechanics. July 1951. Photographer not known

Helen and Jackie Stewart in Saint Jean-Cap-Ferrat. May 1966. Photograph by Victor Blackman
Opposite: Graham Hill in Monaco. May 1966. Photograph by Victor Blackman

Coupe des Petites Cylindres at Reims.
July 1948. Photographer not known

Henry Seagrave before leaving for Daytona Beach, Florida, where he set a land speed record of 203.79 mph.
February 1927. Photograph by E. Bacon

Kaye Don's 4000 hp 'Silver Bullet' outside the Sunbeam factory. February 1930. Photographer not known

Jack Brabham (Brabham-Honda) drives through a cloudburst at the Montjuich Circuit in Barcelona. April 1966. Photographer not known

Opposite: Reg Parnell (Thinwall Special Ferrari) in a hailstorm at Silverstone. May 1951. Photographer not known

Donald Campbell in the cockpit of his father's new 'Bluebird' car in Horley, Surrey.
January 1933. Photographer not known

Opposite: Mr Woppit, Donald Campbell's mascot, accompanies him on a test run in 'Bluebird'
on Lake Eyre salt flats, South Australia. May 1964. Photographer not known

Peter C. T. Clark and Marcus Chambers'
HRG mechanics repair tyres and brew up
at Le Mans. June 1938.
Photograph by Horace Abrahams

Joseph Paul's Delage crashes in the JCC International Trophy Race at Brooklands. May 1938. Photographer not known

Brooklands. Circa 1908. Photographer not known

Escalier (Jaguar XK120) on the second day of the Rallye International des Alpes.
August 1953. Photographer not known

Opposite: Unknown driver (Ferrari) during the Rallye International des Alpes.
August 1953. Photograph by Rodolfo Mailander

Bob Ansell (ERA) refuels at Donington. June 1939. Photographer not known

Woolf Barnato and Bernard Rubin's Bentley refuels at Le Mans. June 1928. Photographer not known

Mechanics work on Fangio's Mercedes W196 at the French Grand Prix in Reims.
July 1954. Photograph by Joseph McKeown

Opposite: Karl Kling and Juan Manuel Fangio at Silverstone.
July 1954. Photograph by Terry Disney

Dennis Scribbons (ERA-B)
hangs on to his broken
exhaust pipe in the
Coronation Trophy at
Crystal Palace. April 1937.
Photograph by Hudson

Contestant after a 'Junior Grand Prix' in Detroit, Michigan. October 1955. Photographer not known
Opposite: Bruce Carter in his pedal-driven racing car in Edgware. September 1955. Photograph by Reg Speller

The Cadillac Spyder driven by
Briggs Cunningham and Phil Walters in
the Le Mans 24 Hour Race. July 1950.
Photographer not known

John Cooper with the 500cc Formula 3 car he designed with his father.
They used a JAP motorcycle engine mounted behind the cockpit and two Fiat Topolino
half-chassis joined end-to-end. Circa 1951. Photographer not known

Opposite: A Cooper Formula 2 emerges before a race at Brands Hatch.
May 1951. Photographer not known

RAC International Car Race on the Isle of Man. June 1937. Photographer not known

Tourist Trophy at Ards, Northern Ireland. August 1930. Photographer not known

David Bruce-Brown (Fiat S74) and co-driver before the
Grand Prix de l'Automobile Club de France. 1912. Photographer not known

Opposite: Circuit des Ardennes. 1907. Photographer not known

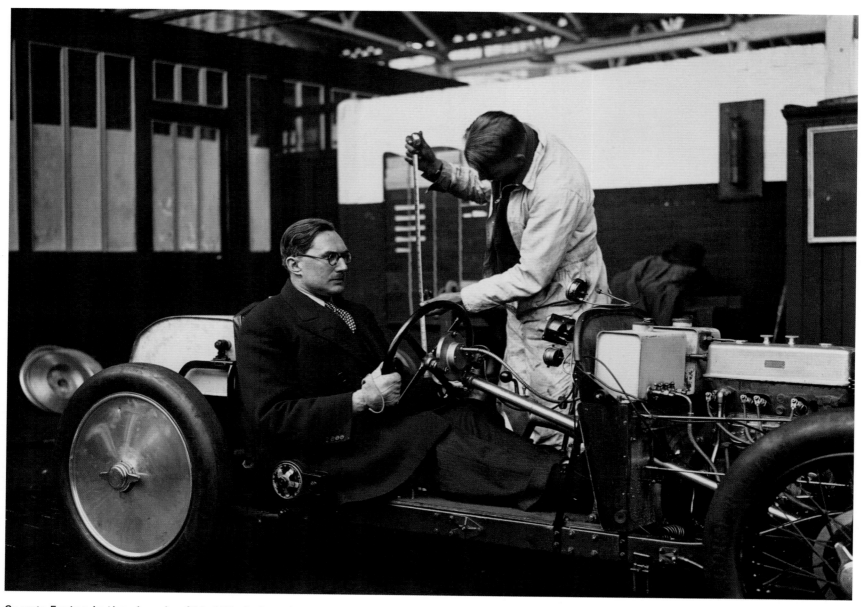

George Eyston in the chassis of his MG, designed to break speed records. January 1932. Photographer not known

Opposite: The frame of Eyston's 'Thunderbolt'. August 1937. Photographer not known

Damon Hill, aged 6, uses a periscope to watch his father race at Silverstone. July 1967. Photograph by Victor Blackman

Opposite: Graham Hill. May 1965. Photographer not known

Gilberte Thirion and Annie Bousquet (Gordini T155) in the Mille Miglia. May 1954. Photograph by Rodolfo Mailander

Miss G. Bucknell and Miss D. Bucknell at the Women's Motor Trial held in Barnet. July 1930. Photographer not known

Christian Werner (Mercedes PP) in the Targa Florio. This is the only time that the Mercedes team ran with their cars painted red. During practice the highly partisan local Sicilians rolled boulders in front of cars not painted red. Team manager Alfred Neubauer had all his cars repainted before the race. April 1924.

Photographer not known

257

Fangio (Alfa Romeo No. 34) passes abandoned cars at the Tabac corner during the Monaco Grand Prix. Ten drivers were involved in collisions when spray from the harbour soaked the track on the first lap. May 1950. Photograph by Rodolfo Mailander

Opposite: Fangio celebrates victory in the Monaco Grand Prix. May 1950. Photograph by Rodolfo Mailander

**Malcolm Campbell
with his new 'Bluebird'.
January 1935.**
Photographer not known

George Abecassis (ALTA) at the Sydenham Trophy meeting at Crystal Palace. May 1938. Photograph by H. F. Davis

Unidentified driver (Aston Martin). September 1935. Photographer not known

Mike Hawthorn with his new nylon crash helmet. July 1957. Photographer not known

Opposite: Phil Hill (Ferrari Dino 246) retires from the Portuguese Grand Prix.
August 1960. Photographer not known

Louis 'Sabipa' Charavel's Bugatti T39A
lands in a garden 50 feet below
the road after he skidded to avoid
a boulder during the Targa Florio
in Sicily. April 1927.
Photographer not known

Refuelling at Brooklands. Circa 1907. Photographer not known

Jack Dunfee at the Brooklands petrol station. July 1929. Photographer not known

The Ferrari team at Zandvoort for the Dutch Grand Prix. Left to right: Giuseppe Farina,
Nello Ugolini (team manager), Alberto Ascari and Luigi Villoresi. June 1953. Photographer not known

Opposite: Luigi Villoresi at Silverstone. August 1952. Photograph by Ronald Startup

Joan Richmond (Ballot) at Brooklands.
March 1934. Photograph by Douglas Miller

Opposite: Kay Petre (Austin) at Brooklands.
October 1937. Photographer not known

Stirling Moss (BRM P25) is disqualified for receiving assistance when he push-starts after spinning during the French Grand Prix at Reims. July 1959. Photographer not known

Consalvo Sanesi (Alfa Romeo 159) pushes his car across the line to finish 10th in the French Grand Prix at Reims. July 1952. Photographer not known

A casualty awaiting first aid is laid on a car, after 6 people are killed and 30 injured when Armando Garcia Cifuentes crashes into the crowd at the Cuban Grand Prix in Havana. February 1958.

277

The Browns Lane team are ready with the Stirling Moss/Norman Dewis Jaguar C-Type for the Mille Miglia. May 1952. Photographer not known

Tony Dennis' Jaguar D-Type after the Easter Monday meeting at Goodwood. April 1956. Photographer not known

Fangio (Mercedes W196) passes
team manager Alfred Neubauer
during the Argentinian Grand Prix
in Buenos Aires. January 1955.
Photographer not known

John Hodge in his MG L2 Magna. May 1934. Photographer not known

Opposite: Graham Whitehead after his only Formula 1 race in the British Grand Prix at Silverstone. July 1952. Photograph by Stroud

E. S. and R. S. Sneath (Sunbeam Talbot) undertake the Épreuve de Regularité in Monaco during the Monte Carlo Rally. January 1952.
Photographer not known

Reg Parnell's Aston Martin DB3 catches fire during refuelling at Goodwood. August 1952. Photographer not known

Opposite: Keith Ballisat and Claude Dubois (Sunbeam Tiger Ford) retire with engine problems at Le Mans. June 1964. Photographer not known

Muriel Thompson is the winning driver in the blindfold competition
at Brooklands. July 1911. Photographer not known

Opposite: Elsie 'Bill' Wisdom practises for the Double Twelve Hour Race
at Brooklands. May 1931. Photographer not known

**Brooklands from the air.
May 1938.**
Photographer not known

Count Carlo Felice Trossi at Montlhery for the French Grand Prix.
July 1934. Photographer not known

Opposite: Guy Moll (Alfa Romeo Tipo-B P3) after winning the Monaco Grand Prix.
April 1934. Photographer not known

Stirling Moss at Bonneville salt flats before a land speed record attempt. May 1957. Photographer not known

Engineer Leo Villa talks to Donald Campbell after testing 'Bluebird' at Goodwood. July 1960. Photographer not known

100 Miles High Speed Reliability Trials at Brooklands.
May 1925. Photograph by MacGregor

Giuseppe Campari (Alfa Romeo) during the Ulster Grand Prix. August 1931. Photographer not known

Opposite: Maserati mechanics at Silverstone. July 1954. Photograph by Stroud

H. M. Walters designed and built his 350cc
single-cylinder kick-start engine Jappic. 1925.
Photographer not known

301

Prince 'Bira' Birabongse Bhanudej Bhanuban (ERA) wins the London Grand Prix. July 1937. Photographer not known

Opposite: Prince Bira at the Manx Cup in Douglas, Isle of Man. August 1947. Photographer not known

Spectators in the pits at Amiens for the French Grand Prix.
July 1913. Photographer not known

Opposite: Albert Guyot and Louis Wagner's
Rolland Pilain A22s before the French Grand Prix at Strasbourg.
July 1922. Photographer not known

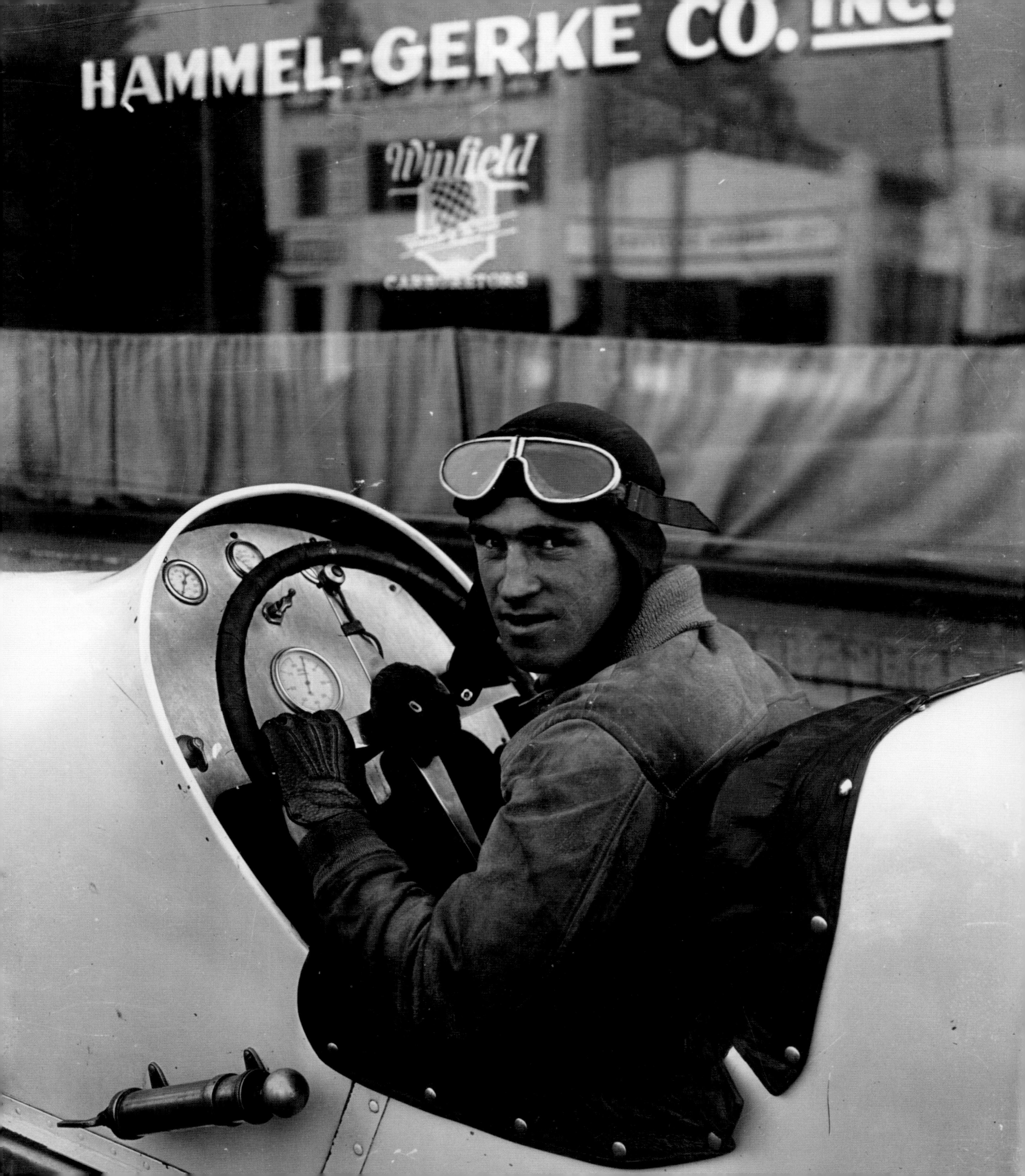
HAMMEL-GERKE CO. INC.
Winfield

J. Chance in his Enfield-Alldays. October 1921. Photograph by W. J. Brunell

Opposite: 'Shorty' Cantlon, in his Miller Schofield, winner of the AAA National Championship
at Akron, Ohio. June 1930. Photographer not known

Hotelier and garage proprietor Jack Field has bought Kaye Don's Sunbeam 'Silver Bullet' and has entered Southport Motor Club's speed trials. 1934.
Photographer not known

Ces 3 champions du monde ont choisi la "JAGUAR"

Frère au volant de la Jaguar XK 120 c.

French promotion for the
Jaguar XK120 C-Type. Circa 1952.
Photographer not known

Mercedes throw a party for Peter Collins and Stirling Moss
(standing behind car) to celebrate their victory in the Targa Florio.
October 1955. Photographer not known

Opposite: Peter Collins (Mercedes 300SLR) restarts after a pit stop during
the Targa Florio in Sicily. October 1955. Photographer not known

Fay Taylour after practice at Crystal Palace Speedway. June 1934. Photograph by Harry Todd

A Brooklands mechanic fastens Miss D. Turner's crash helmet. July 1937. Photographer not known

The winning Bentley Speed Six team that took first, second, third and fourth place at Le Mans. Left to right: Jack Dunfee and Glen Kidston (no. 9), Woolf Barnato and Sir Henry 'Tim' Birkin (no. 1), Frank Clement and Jean Chassagne (no. 8) and John Benjafield and Baron André d'Erlanger (no. 10). June 1929.
Photographer not known

Stirling Moss (ERA G-Type) at Silverstone. August 1952. Photograph by Ronald Startup

Opposite: Mercedes mechanics at the French Grand Prix in Reims. July 1954. Photograph by Joseph McKeown

Jules Foresti in his Djelmo before a land speed record attempt at Pendine Sands, Carmarthen. November 1927. Photograph by L. Blandford

Foresti's Djelmo after his record attempt at Pendine Sands, Carmarthen. November 1927. Photographer not known

The Stutz pit signals a change of spark plugs at
Le Mans. June 1929. Photographer not known

D. Z. Ferranti waits in his Austin while Southport Motor Club members discuss whether the blizzard conditions will prevent racing at Birkdale, Merseyside. February 1931.
Photographer not known

The Vanderbilt Cup at Milwaukee. 1912. Photographer not known

The Gordon Bennett Trophy at Athy, County Kildare. 1903. Photographer not known

Stirling Moss (BRP Lotus) crashes at
Goodwood. April 1962.
Photograph by Victor Blackman

Members' Bridge hairpin at Brooklands.
July 1935. Photographer not known

331

Tazio Nuvolari with his Alfa Romeo. August 1920. Photographer not known

Benito Mussolini at the wheel of Nuvolari's Alfa Romeo. Circa 1932. Photographer not known

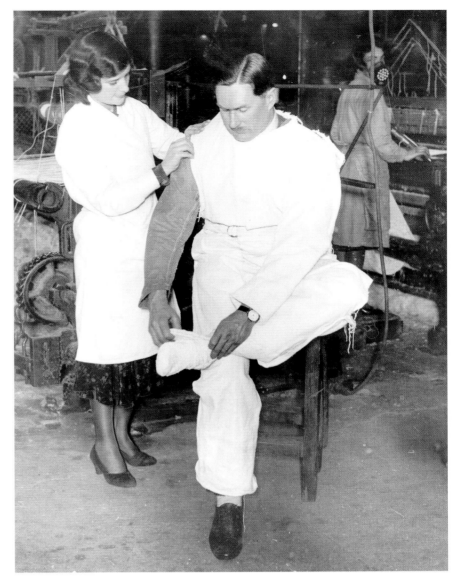

George Eyston has a fitting for a fire-retardant asbestos suit and socks. January 1932. Photographer not known

Opposite: George Eyston in his 7-ton, 73-litre, twin-Rolls-Royce aero-engined 'Thunderbolt'. February 1936. Photographer not known

Donald Campbell starts a model car race at the Manor House School. February 1931. Photographer not known

Opposite: Sand racetrack for toy cars on the beach at Bognor Regis. August 1939. Photograph by Quinn

Jaguar mechanics at Le Mans. June 1953. Photograph by Ronald Startup

Opposite: Mike Hawthorn at Monza. July 1953. Photograph by David Lees

A. H. 'Lindsay' Eccles (3.3 Type 59 Bugatti) passes the timekeeper's hut at Brooklands. May 1935. Photographer not known

Jochen Rindt demonstrates Nikon long lens technology to Richie Ginther.
Circa 1969. Photographer not known

Opposite: A keen fan at the Nurburgring. Circa 1965. Photographer not known

The Bentley Speed Six pit at Le Mans. June 1930.
Photographer not known

Bertram 'Bunny' Marshall (Brescia Bugatti) in the International 1500 Trophy
on the Isle of Man. June 1922. Photographer not known

Opposite: Prince Bira follows Cyril Paul (both ERA) into Willaston Corner during
the Manx Car Race on the Isle of Man. May 1936. Photograph by Maeers

Mr Monday's Leyland and
Pat Driscoll's Austin Seven. August
1935. Photograph by R. Wesley

Jack Brabham wins the British Grand Prix at Brands Hatch.
July 1966. Photographer not known

Opposite: Brabham collapses after pushing his Cooper T51 Climax across the
line to finish fourth in the United States Grand Prix, and win the World Championship.
December 1959. Photographer not known

Major Henry Seagrave's 'Golden Arrow' at Daytona Beach, Florida. March 1929. Photographer not known

'Golden Arrow' is driven through London to be put on display in Selfridges department store. April 1929. Photographer not known

Project leader Raymond Mays
presents a model of the
prototype BRM V16 to the BRM
Trust committee. May 1950.
Photograph by Haywood Magee

354

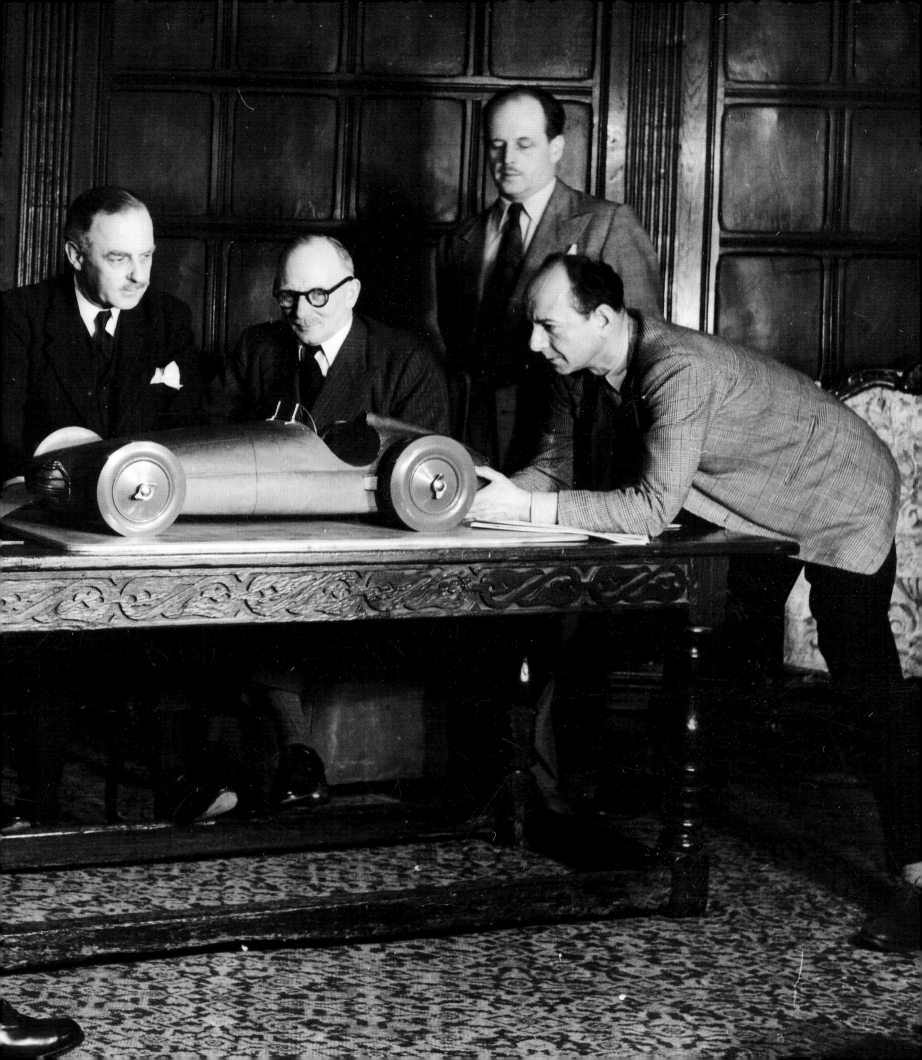

Henri Louveau's Lago-Talbot T26 C in the Swiss Grand Prix at Bremgarten. May 1951. Photographer not known

Opposite: Peter Braid's 500cc Cooper MkIII at the Blandford Formula 3 Race. August 1949. Photographer not known

The start of the Sao Paulo Grand Prix.
March 1948. Photographer not known

Stirling Moss (Rob Walker Lotus 18 Climax) at the Station hairpin during the Monaco Grand Prix. May 1961. Photographer not known

Opposite: Prince Rainier and Princess Grace present the winner's trophy to Stirling Moss at the Monaco Grand Prix. May 1960. Photographer not known

D. H. Perring fixes an RAC pennant to his Triumph before a rally in Torquay. April 1939. Photographer not known

Major J. A. Driscoll (in fur coat) with his crew before setting off for the Monte Carlo Rally. January 1934. Photographer not known

Hans Stuck (Auto Union C-Type) during the
Hungarian Grand Prix at Nepliget Park, Budapest.
June 1936. Photographer not known

Painting the starting lines at Brooklands. March 1936. Photograph by Reg Speller

Opposite: Ground staff preparing the track for the Easter meeting at Brooklands. March 1929. Photographer not known

J. B. Marquis (Sunbeam) at 'Death Curve' during the International Grand Prix at Santa Monica. March 1914. Photographer not known

Eddie Pullen (Mercer) at 'Death Curve' during the Vanderbilt Cup at Santa Monica. April 1914. Photographer not known

Stirling Moss gets into his MGX 181, an experimental car developed by the British Motor Corporation, at Bonneville salt flats. July 1957. Photographer not known

Opposite: The oil guideline used by drivers on Bonneville salt flats. Circa 1960s. Photographer not known

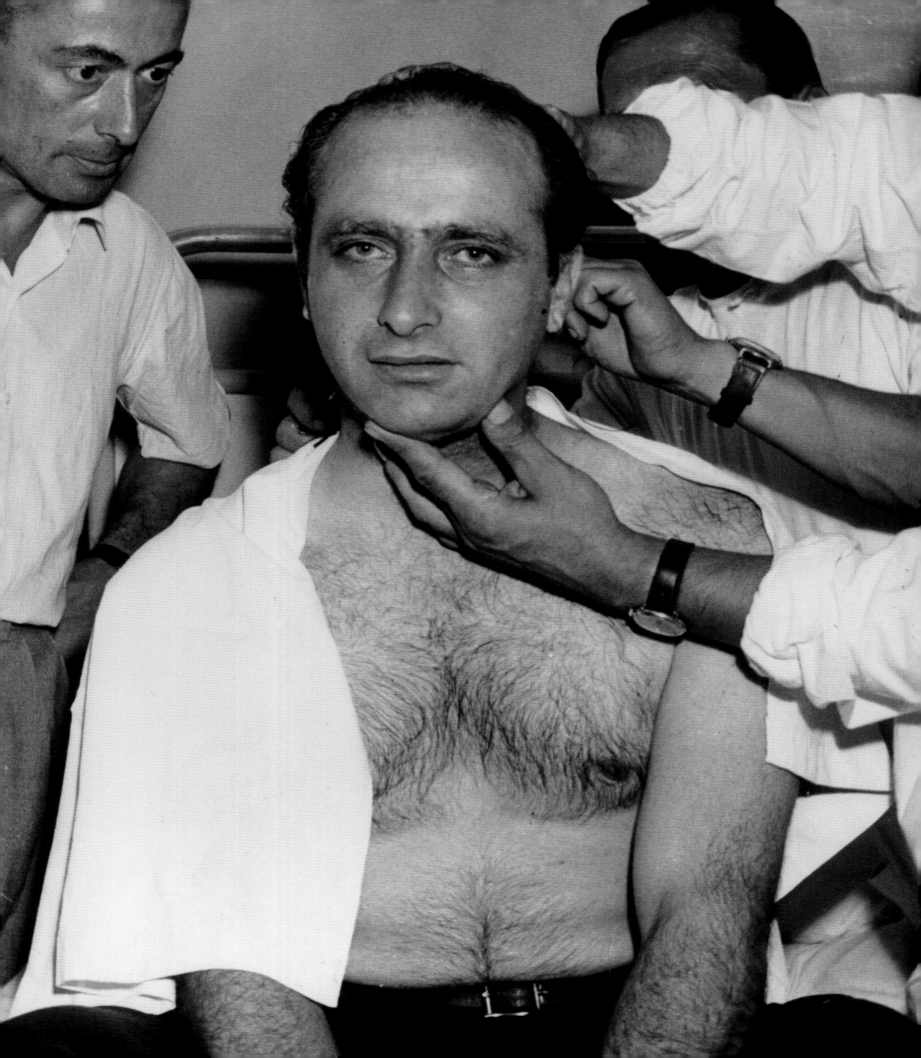

Fangio wins the Italian Grand Prix at Monza. September 1953. Photographer not known

Opposite: Fangio is examined after doctors remove the plaster from his neck, which was broken when he crashed in a race nearly a year before. September 1952. Photographer not known

Alberto Ascari's Ferrari 375 after practice for the Italian Grand Prix at Monza. September 1951.
Photograph by Rodolfo Mailander

Jackie Stewart at Watkins Glen.
October 1971.
Photograph by Karl Ludvigsen

INDEX

PHOTOGRAPHIC CREDITS

Endpapers: The bonnet of Juan Manuel Fangio's Mercedes W196 STR during preparations for the British Grand Prix at Silverstone. July 1954.
Photograph by J. Wilds

ACKNOWLEDGEMENTS

For Julie.

My special thanks to Nick Culpeper, Mark Debnam, Jack Tennant and Lisa Thiel for the benefit of their wisdom throughout this project.

Thanks also to the following people for their patience, support and expertise:

Alan Ashby, Marcel Ashby, Gordon Burn, Julia Carmichael, Ian Crane, Madelaine Debnam, Alice Goater, George Goater, Nick Goater, David Godwin, Carol Gorner, Ken Griffiths, Will Griffiths, Steve Guise, Kim Harman, Suzanne Hodgart, David Hodgkinson, Shem Law, Jen Little, Michael Loffler, Lindsay Marriott, David Montgomery, Rex Needle, Rich Pearce, Michelle Pickering, Polly Powell, Michael Rand, Peter Campbell Saunders, Sir Jackie Stewart OBE, Camilla Stoddart, Sally Taylor and my Mum & Dad.

From Cassell Illustrated:

Liz Fowler, Gabrielle Mander and Adam Smith.

From picture sources:

Jonathan Hamston and Nicole Newman at Corbis.
Emily Lewis at EMPICS.
Bob Ahern, John Anderson, Liz Ihre, Jennifer Jeffries, Tea McAleer, Charles Merullo and Sarah Parkinson at Getty Images.
Anders Clausager and Karam Ram at the Jaguar Daimler Heritage Trust.
Peter Higham, Kevin Wood and Tim Wright at LAT.
Karl Ludvigsen and Sam Turner at the Ludvigsen Library.
Jonathan Day and Tim Woodcock at the National Motor Museum, Beaulieu.
Neill Bruce at Neill Bruce's Automobile Photolibrary.

All motoring companies and organisations who helped with caption detail, particularly:

John Pulford at the Brooklands Museum.
Julie Bate and John Bridcutt at the Bugatti Trust.
Silvia Pini at Ferrari.
Sue Filmer at the History of Advertising Trust.
Diana Jones and Roger Sims at the Manx Museum.
Donn Gurney at Race Legends Inc.